It Happened to ME
Runaway

Interviews by Angela Neustatter and Helen Elliott
Photography by Laurence Cendrowicz

W
FRANKLIN WATTS
LONDON • SYDNEY

© 2003 Franklin Watts

First published in Great Britain by
Franklin Watts
96 Leonard Street
London
EC2A 4XD

Franklin Watts Australia
45-51 Huntley Street
Alexandria
NSW 2015

ISBN: 0 7496 4336 6

A CIP record for this book is available from the British Library.

Printed in Malaysia

Series editor: Sarah Peutrill
Art director: Jonathan Hair
Design: Steve Prosser
Photographs: Laurence Cendrowicz (unless otherwise stated)

Picture credits: Paul Baldesare/Photofusion: 4, 18, 22, 38. Matt
Hammill 24, 25, 26, 29, 30. Bob Watkins/Photofusion: 44.
All Photofusion photographs posed by models. Whilst every
attempt has been made to clear copyright should there be any
inadvertent omission please apply in the first instance to the
publisher regarding rectification.

With grateful thanks to our interviewees and Camden Under-25s
Advice Centre, Barnardo's Missing in Yorkshire Service and The
Salvation Army.

Contents

Introduction

Mention the word 'runaway' and many people think of Huck Finn and Tom Sawyer having fun on the Mississippi River. But the life of a runaway can often be less like an adventure novel and more like a horror story - sleeping on the streets, not knowing where the next meal is coming from and being at risk from abuse.

Who runs away?

Young runaways come from all sections of society, regardless of wealth, ethnicity or geographical area. Many may have got on well with their parents and step-parents, but find that a change in circumstances resulted in a crisis, and they were forced to leave or they ran away. Children living in stepfamilies or in care, in particular, are at an increased risk of running away. However, the most significant factor in who runs away is not the family structure itself, but the quality of the relationship between the child and the parents or carers.

One of the key things that children who run away say is that they have not been listened to by the adults in their life. They feel that their views and concerns are not taken seriously.

Where do runaways go?

Some stay with another relative or friend, but many find themselves on the streets, or in hostels or bed-and-breakfast accommodation.

Why is it an increasing problem?

The problems that cause many young people to run away - family break-ups, drug and alcohol abuse in their homes - have increased in the past 15 years. At the same time the community is less involved. In the past, a young adult who was being abused or had other problems at home could turn to neighbours. But this support is less likely to be there today. Young adults can find that there are few adults to turn to, and no safe places to go.

Why do children run away?

There are many reasons why young people run away from home but it is usually a desperate cry for help. Here are some of the reasons they give:

◆ school problems, such as bullying, truancy, exam results, problems with teachers and pressure to achieve;
◆ disagreements over lifestyle such as boyfriends or girlfriends, clothes and staying out late;
◆ personal issues, such as relations with parents and step-parents, pregnancy, sexual orientation, physical, sexual or emotional abuse, the death of a friend or relative, drug or alcohol problems, or getting into trouble with the police;
◆ worries that they feel they just can't talk to their parents or carers about. They may fear parents will be angry, not interested, too busy or just won't understand.

Do you know someone who is thinking about running away? Or are you thinking about running away yourself? If so - read this first!

Think before you run

♦ It may seem you're on your own and there's no one you can turn to, but whatever your problem there are things you can do and people who can help.
♦ You can start by talking to your parents or carers. Tell them that you are worried or upset and want to talk to them about it. Try to be as calm as you can and explain what is bothering you. Problems can often be resolved in this way. You could also speak to your teacher or doctor.
♦ Try to put yourself in your parents' or carers' position and look at things from their point of view, too. Arguments over things like staying out late can be resolved. On the one hand, you need to understand that your parents are probably worried about you getting home safely. At the same time they need to understand that you are growing up and want to be more independent.

What about my friend?

♦ If a friend is thinking about running away, try talking to them about their problems. You might suggest they speak to a teacher, social worker, doctor or one of the organisations listed on page 46. If you think your friend will actually run away, talk to a teacher yourself – it might stop them making a mistake.

Is running away the answer?

♦ There's nothing glamorous about life on the streets. It can be cold, dirty and very dangerous. You could end up feeling hungry, lonely and scared.

It Happened to Jamie

Jamie, 19, ran away from his home in Scotland when he was 14 after being beaten up by his stepmother. He lives at a Salvation Army hostel in Bristol.

6

Q Did you live with both parents as a child?

A My mum and dad split up when I was two so I hardly remember life with them as a couple. Together with my sister, who is a year younger than me, I went to live with my mother but that only lasted until I was five as she had a nervous breakdown. My father said it was because she was on drugs. She said it was because she was on her own with two children and trying to do a university degree.

Q So what happened to you then?

A We went to live with my dad and my stepmother. At first I was happy and excited because I was a boy and liked the idea of being with my father, and my stepmother was nice as pie. She had two children of her own who seemed nice too.

Q So that was a happy arrangement?

A Not for long. After about two weeks my stepmother started to pick

It's a Fact that...

22 per cent of young people living in stepfamilies run away, although for many it is for just a short time, and to another member of their family.

on me and my sister. Niggly stuff but it made me anxious about everything I did. Then she started slapping me when I did things she didn't like, not very often at first, but it built up over the years. Slaps turned into real beatings, and over really trivial things like taking a biscuit.

Q Didn't your father try to defend you?

A I don't think he really noticed. My father drank all the time. He was a bouncer in a nightclub and had a lot of opportunity to get drunk. He never gave me and my sister birthday presents or anything, and I don't remember him being affectionate.

Q Did you see your mother at all?

A I hardly ever saw my mother because my

stepmother didn't want it. Mum sent me birthday cards and money over the years but they never reached me. One day she came to the house - she was crying, but she was sent away. I was about eight at the time. It was six years before I saw her again.

Q Did things get easier as you got older?

A No. I lived in fear of my stepmother's beatings and people knew it was going on. Her children, who got away with murder, felt sorry for us but it didn't help. Only my stepgran stuck up for me when she was there. Then one day when my stepmother was hitting my sister with a hard slipper my sister kicked her and my stepmother fell over. I was 13 at the time and I called her a stupid cow.

Q What happened then?

A My stepmother set about really beating me. She beat my head against a light switch on the wall and I fell down and was concussed. But when I came to, I punched her like I would a man and she fell down.

Q What did you do then?

A I ran out of the house and stayed overnight with a mate who knew how bad things were. The next day my auntie came over and took me to my father's house to get clothes while my stepmother was at work, then she took me to my mother's house. My mother

> " I lived in fear of my stepmother's beatings and people knew it was going on. "

7

was really pleased to see me. She explained that she had wanted to see me but wasn't able to. I thought I'd be able to live with her, but not long after I arrived her boyfriend accused me of stealing money from his wallet. In fact my mum had taken the money and forgotten, but I just knew it wasn't going to work staying there.

Q So what did you do?

A I went to live with my gran on my mum's side. I'd been going to school but she encouraged me not to because she was drinking and could use my £2 a day tuck money for drink. So I used to have a bunch of mates around during the day and we'd sit around and watch movies. Nobody at

> " Nobody at school seemed to notice. There were no reports of me being truant."

school seemed to notice. There were no reports of me being truant.

Q Were you happy living with your grandmother?

A Not really, and I fairly soon drifted off to another town where I had friends and I was able to stay some nights with them. I started drinking and smoking cannabis, taking ecstasy, valium and temazepam. I was blocking out all the bad feelings and getting through time. When I didn't have anywhere to stay I walked around all night. I stole stuff out of cars to get money.

Q Did you get on to hard drugs?

A A friend introduced me to smack. I was really sick,

but afterwards I got the best night's sleep ever and I wanted more. I was hooked because smack made me feel invincible. I just wasn't scared of anything.

Q How did you feel about your mother and father at this time?

A I didn't stay in touch with my mum and dad and I didn't miss them. I had mates who helped me with clothes and food and money. I didn't hang out with other runaways. But I did stay in touch with my gran.

Q Didn't you get lonely?

A I met a Chinese friend and worked in his father's shop to help out. I lived with him and his father for two years. We were both using a lot of drugs, including heroin. But things went wrong because he fell out with his father and I had to find somewhere else to go.

Q Where did you go after that?

A I was 17 by this time and I met a woman of 39 in a pub. I told her I was 27 and I went to live with her for about a year. She really cared for me and was like a mother figure in many ways. I only did smack at weekends then, but my girlfriend who was a nurse never knew. She hated drugs. But then I caught her cheating on me with somebody else and I was devastated. It was the first time I'd been in love. I slapped her in the mouth and then went. It was so painful I can hardly talk about it even now.

Q When that relationship finished where did you go?

A I really didn't know what to do with myself then so I went back to my home town, but to nothing. I was technically homeless even though my family were there. I saw my auntie one day. She told me to go and live with my mother and get myself off smack. She paid for my ticket to Bristol, bought me new clothes and shoes.

Q Did you do that?

A My mother didn't have a place for me. I got into bed and breakfast through the Hub (an agency for single homeless people) but in that

"I didn't stay in touch with my mum and dad and I didn't miss them."

9

It's a Fact that...

One third of children who ran away from stepfamilies said they had been forced to leave home.

Running away is more common in stepfamilies but this is probably due to the fact that the child runs to their other family.

place I was accused of supplying Class A drugs which killed someone. It wasn't me but of course I had to leave. I met a mate who was homeless and I became homeless with him. We slept behind a fast-food restaurant.

Q So things were going downhill for you?

A I was in a bad state. I began shoplifting because I

> **" I met a mate who was homeless and I became homeless with him. "**

needed money for smack and it meant I didn't have to beg. Then I got caught. I was sent to Horfield Prison for two weeks to detox and to another prison for three months.

Q Did you feel you had reached rock bottom?

A In fact I mixed quite well with the boys there and I got the best prison job preparing and serving meals. I pestered the wardens until I got it. While I was in prison I got to watch TV in my cell. I went to the gym every other day. It was the first time I'd been to a gym. In the evening I socialised with other inmates. In fact prison was a bit of a sanctuary. There was a routine, you were fed, you had somewhere to sleep and people to talk to.

Of course it was loss of freedom, but my freedom hadn't been such fun. So it wasn't that bad. But I was lucky to be in an easy-going prison.

Q You detoxed in prison so did you stay clean when you came out?

A No. The probation service got me a place in a Salvation Army hostel. Although they give you a key worker, who keeps an eye on you and is there if you have a problem, and a breakfast is provided, you are on your own for the rest of the day. I went into town and was immediately mixing with my mates and using smack again. But my key worker at the hostel is preparing me now to do one of their detox programmes because I really want to get off the stuff for good.

Q So how long have you lived at the hostel and what do you do with your time?

A I've stayed here about three months and I have a routine for the days. I go to the gym. I see my probation officer every two

"I think I'll stay here ... there are people I call friends."

weeks and for the rest I do what I do in town. I don't work because I'd lose my benefit but also I can't until I've detoxed. I think I'll stay here because I do feel my key worker cares about me and there are people I call friends. Sometimes I do feel it's a bit like a family. On my birthday I wondered if I'd get any presents. I didn't - but then that's how it was when I had a family. ■

Talking Points

◆ Statistically children who live with step-parents are more likely to be runaways. Why do you think this is? With stepfamilies becoming increasingly common, how do you think children like Jamie can be protected?

◆ Do you think hostels and bed and breakfasts are a good way to keep young runaways off the streets?

It Happened to Ajirun

Ajirun ran away from home when she was 16. She had been taken to Bangladesh by her father where he tried to pressurise her into marrying a cousin. Now, aged 18, she lives in a rented flat in East London.

Q Who did you grow up with?

A I never knew my real mother, who died of cancer when I was a baby, and my old man never talked about her. My mother died leaving me, my twin brother and my two sisters. My father remarried quickly. My stepmother then had children and I never felt she really cared for me much.

Q So was your father the one who gave you affection?

A Not at all. I made breakfast for him before going to school and supper in the evening. And sometimes he would call me down after I'd gone to bed at night-time to look after him. But he wasn't

It's a Fact that...

Most young people who leave home do so only briefly. Around two thirds of runaways stay in their local area, one in five run to the nearest city while one in seven go further afield.

kind to me. I felt he liked my elder sister much better.

Q So do you have happy memories of childhood?

A Honestly I don't. I was very lonely and my stepmother kept herself to herself. I never got close to her. It's always seemed to me that getting close to people is dangerous: someone always gets hurt.

Q Was there anywhere you felt cared about?

A School was the place I was happiest. The teachers were very kind to me and they understood that things were difficult at home. My twin brother was at school with me and the teachers learned a bit about what went on at home. They let me know they were there to offer support if I wanted it.

Q So did you do well at school in spite of being unhappy at home?

A Yes. I liked studying and I got good marks, but then when I was 13 my old man decided to take us all back to Bangladesh where he came from. I didn't want to go but felt I had to.

Q So did you enjoy seeing your country of origin once you were there?

A I don't know if I would have enjoyed it if I'd been allowed some freedom, but as soon as we arrived my old man told my sisters and me that he wanted us to marry. The person he wanted me to marry was a cousin, and it wasn't a choice, or a question of whether we even liked the men he had chosen, this was

just what we were supposed to do. I put up a big fight and told my old man I wasn't going to marry.

Q So did he accept that?

A Not at all. We stayed two years in Bangladesh and through all that time he bullied me and tried to force me into marriage. He even found someone to try to hypnotise me, but I managed to resist that. He didn't need to beat me because I was marooned in this place and I had no idea how I could escape. I was terribly miserable and sometimes it was hard not to give in. My sisters did as my old man wanted and got married but I had seen what life was like for women in Bangladeshi marriages. I was determined that, no matter what, I

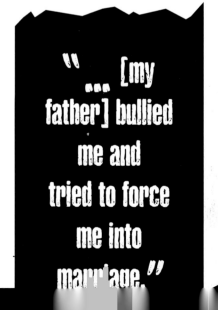

" ... [my father] bullied me and tried to force me into marriage."

13

didn't want that. It was very lucky that my elder brother said he was returning to the UK and my old man decided we would all come back.

Q So were you able to return to school then?

A I hadn't been to school at all in Bangladesh so in a way I didn't want to go back because I thought I'd be so behind. But I also realised that I needed to get GCSEs if I was going to succeed in life. So I went back to school and in fact I caught up with the work very quickly. I got nine GCSEs when I left at 16. The teachers were really

> **" I don't like talking about things. I prefer to keep my troubles to myself."**

It's a Fact that...

Young runaways come from all sections of society, irrespective of wealth, ethnicity or geographical area. The most significant factor is the quality of relationship between the child and his or her parents.

kind to me and made it plain they were pleased to have me in the school. But things were still very difficult at home. I was getting more and more miserable because my old man was very angry with me for opposing him. Then one day the cousin I was supposed to marry came over and there was a massive row with my old man and my older brother turning on me and saying I should marry. I felt my brother had really turned against me and he said a lot of very nasty things to me.

Q So what did you do about that?

A I decided I would go. I didn't tell anyone but I packed a few things and just walked out when nobody was around. I thought, I'm going and that's it. I won't be coming back.

Q Did you have any idea where you would go?

A I went to a place called Dame Collett House in Stepney, London, because my teachers had said to me that if I ever needed help I should go there. They were very kind. They sorted out a hostel place for me where the people were understanding and very nice to me. I had a room to myself, which felt very good because I wanted some private space. They offered counselling but I didn't want it. I don't like talking about things. I prefer to keep my troubles to myself.

Q Were there other people like you there?

A There were a lot of people who had run away

from home there. Some my age but quite a lot older - married and divorced women who had domestic troubles and were frightened of their partners. Some helped me a lot and I am still friends with them. There's a woman with two children I still go and stay with.

Q Did your family know where you were and did they try to get in touch with you?

A I told my twin brother where I was. He was worried about me, but he knew I was happier. I didn't communicate with anyone else in my family and nobody bothered.

Q Did you stay in the hostel?

A I left that hostel after a couple of months because it was quite expensive and I

was sick a lot so I couldn't work. I stayed with a couple of friends for a while but you can't do that for too long. Someone told me about another hostel in Bethnal Green and I was happy to go there. The Queen came down once to see the place and she shook my hand. There were a lot of girls who had been through bad experiences and had run away from them, and some who had ended up on the streets. I made good friends there too, and that place became like a home. I was living on benefits and I could just afford it.

Q So how did you spend your days?

A I did courses in drama, drama theory and travel and tourism. One of my teachers who knew I wanted to travel gave me the name of organisations which help students get placements in the developing world. I wrote to about 50 of them but I wasn't getting much luck. Then I went to summer university in Whitechapel.

" Someone told me about another hostel ... I was happy to go there. "

It's a Fact that...

41 per cent of young runaways have been excluded (expelled) from school.

There I met Tony, who runs a small charity called the Daneford Trust. It does cross-cultural exchanges helping kids - often kids from fairly hard-up backgrounds - go to work as volunteers in the developing world. He saw my name on a list and recognised it because his was one of the organisations I had written to. So he came and spoke to me and said he would help me get sponsorship to go abroad with the Daneford Trust. But I didn't really imagine it would be possible for someone like me.

Q So what did you have to do?

A Tony told me that I needed to write to big organisations asking if they would sponsor me to go and teach in the Caribbean. I was amazed because I raised the money very quickly. I went to St. Vincent and stayed there six months teaching children. It was a wonderful experience because I felt needed and valuable there and I belonged.

Q But how was it when you got back to England?

A I got my hostel place back and the Daneford Trust was still there to help me. I continue to work for them on the administrative side as a volunteer when I have time. Tony and the others working there have become like my family. My own family are now in Bangladesh and I hear nothing. I have a job, a home that I rent, and I am feeling good about myself. ∎

Talking Points

◆ Why do you think some parents organise arranged marriages? Do parents know best?

◆ Why do you think a lot of runaways end up in London? What do you think the attraction is?

◆ What ways has Ajirun used to move on in her life? What might other runaways learn from this story?

It Happened to David

Photographs in this section posed by models.

David* ran away from home in Cheltenham at the age of 17. He'd been continually physically abused by his mother's boyfriend and left after a fight. Since this interview he has run away from the hostel where he was living, having been accused of stealing. [* Not his real name.]

Q What are your memories of early life?

A I grew up in Cheltenham with my mum and dad. I was an only child until my sister was born when I was six. I remember this as a happy time but when I was nine that changed. My father's brother, my favourite uncle - he used to take me fishing and playing rugby - killed himself and that seemed to upset my mum and dad's relationship. Things started going bad and then my dad moved out taking my sister with him. I lost both the important men in my life. It was a bad time.

Q How did family life change after this?

A I was about nine when Dad left and that was bad. Mum had picked me up from school and we came into the house. There on the fridge were two notes - one for me and one for my mum. He just said he'd moved to London, but it was very hard learning something as devastating as this that way. In my note he said, 'Davey, it's not your fault and don't blame your mum. It's my problem. I need to get out.' But none of it made sense.

"There on the fridge were two notes ... [my dad] said he'd moved to London."

Q How did all this affect your behaviour?

A I got really angry. I ripped up the furniture and I refused to go to school for a time. After a while I started hanging around with a crowd, all older than me. There was one, Robbie, who was 18 and he came round to see me and met my mum who was 34 at that time. I didn't realise what was happening, but the next thing I knew they were together as a couple and he had moved into my house. At first it was all right because Robbie still treated me like he was my mate, but after a few months he started trying to behave like my dad. He tried to discipline me and told me what I could and couldn't do and said I was grounded if I disobeyed. It made me very rebellious.

Q So you didn't have an easy relationship with Robbie?

A There was a lot of jealousy between him and me. I wanted my mum's attention and he was getting it. As things went on he began giving me smacks. And then as I got into my teens things deteriorated still more. He began beating me up left, right and centre. I remember one occasion when he asked if I would make him a cup of tea. I gave it to him but it didn't have enough sugar for him so he threw it over me. I ran upstairs but he chased after me, picked me up by the back of the neck and threw me over

19

" ... [Robbie] threw me over the top banister. I fell all the way down to the bottom of the stairs ... "

the top banister. I fell all the way down to the bottom of the stairs, fracturing two ribs and my wrist. I had to go to hospital several times because of the injuries and they knew something was wrong, but I was too scared to tell.

Q Did your mother do anything to protect you?

A She was there when he threw me over the banister but she was scared of him as well. He roughed her up quite a bit. When we were alone together she would break down, crying and saying she was trying to sort things out for me. The trouble was, whenever Robbie had done something like this, a couple of hours later he would apologise, promising it wouldn't happen again. But in fact the beatings went on.

Q Was there anyone to help you cope?

A The best thing that happened was meeting my girlfriend Danielle just before I left school. She was my friend and companion and she understood what I was going through at home. She invited me to her house a lot and it was like a second home. I felt good to be there. She had a positive effect on my family because there were no rows when she came around.

Q So things improved?

A Only for about a year. Then one day Danielle came to see me. She'd been drinking and she told me she was leaving me for someone else. He came to collect her from my house. The next day at 4 o'clock in the morning there was a phone call telling me Danielle had died in a car crash. That was it. The last time I saw her we argued and I couldn't ever make that better. I was torn apart. Really so upset and I started drinking a bit.

Q Were your family sympathetic?

A They were, because everyone liked Danielle and felt touched by her death. And in fact Robbie took me out for a drink a few times to help me. But then I came home

It's a Fact that...

In the UK children who start running away before the age of 11 are nearly three times more likely to be sexually assaulted on the streets and twice as likely to be hit by their parents than older runaways. They are also more likely to sleep rough and be bullied at school.

> **"She'd been drinking and she told me she was leaving me for someone else."**

one night a bit drunk, by myself, and I woke Robbie up. I shouldn't have done that. He came downstairs and started at me straight away. He grabbed me by the throat, swore at me and hit me a couple of times. He nearly broke my nose again (he had broken my nose and jaw in the past) but my mum came down and pulled us apart.

Q Did you think of leaving?

A I hardly slept realising I needed to get out and I just left. I went to the train station. I was planning to go from

Cheltenham to Weston-Super-Mare. I had a little bit of money from agency work and I began to feel quite excited at the idea of a new beginning and standing on my own two feet.

Q Did things work out as you hoped?

A I got off the train in Bristol and liked the look of it so I went to see the Samaritans and explained that I'd run away and why. They sent me to the Salvation Army and I felt a great weight come off me at the idea that I'd be free of Robbie and someone would help me. But it was a shock when I got to the hostel. There were a lot of alcoholics and heroin addicts and I'd never been into anything like that. I was put in a dormitory with three other guys a lot older than me. I woke up in the middle of the night and one was smoking heroin right in my face. You're not allowed to take drugs in the hostel, but I didn't want to tell anyone. I was very relieved, though, when a couple of days later I was given a single room.

Q Did you miss home?

A I missed my mum a lot but I'm glad to be away from home. I have a group of friends who don't do drugs. I think the hostel were concerned to keep me away from the users. I was advised to keep myself to myself. We'll have a few beers at the weekends and we use the Playstation. I've been here since I left home. I'm 19 now.

Q What do you see as the future?

A I can't really see a future. My key worker at the hostel has helped me with housing applications

> " ... I felt a great weight come off me at the idea that I'd be free of Robbie ... "

and I may get a place of my own but then I have to worry about work and how I'll manage. Meanwhile I feel I'm killing time waiting. I find things to do - chatting with mates, walking around town, exercising a bit kicking a ball around. I watch TV. ■

Talking Points

◆ Why do you think David and Robbie's relationship deteriorated so quickly after Robbie moved in?

◆ What is David experiencing at the hostel? Why might staying at a hostel cause as many problems as it solves? What could be done about this?

It Happened to Sophie

Sophie*, an attractive and confident 16-year-old, lives in inner Sydney in a beautiful old house overlooking the harbour. Her father is an architect and her mother a primary teacher. When Sophie was 15 she ran away from home for a period of six weeks. That period dramatically changed everything about her life.
[* Not her real name.]

Q Tell me where you come in the family.

A I'm the first child in the family, the oldest. I've got two younger sisters. They're 10 and 7.

Q When did you run away from home?

A About eight months ago when I was 15.

Q Can you explain why you left?

A I felt as though my parents didn't give me enough freedom. I wanted to go out and party and have a good time and they weren't really happy with that so they tried to prevent me from doing it. I said well, I don't care what you think, I want to do what I want, so I left. I didn't leave on good terms. I just packed up my stuff and left.

Q How did you feel towards your parents?

A Not very happy at all. I just felt as if my parents didn't understand me or where I was coming from. I was very angry.

"I left. I didn't leave on good terms. I just packed up my stuff and left."

Q Were you doing drugs?

A Yeah, I was doing a fair bit. That probably had something to do with it. I was basically just experimenting. And I was in with the wrong crowd and we were all into experimenting and trying different things.

Q How long did you stay away from your parent's house?

A About a month to six weeks.

Q Where did you stay?

A I just stayed anywhere I could, really. Mainly at my friends' places.

Q So you didn't have to sleep on the streets?

A No. I always had a place to stay.

Q What were the places you stayed like?

A I stayed at one particular place quite a bit. The family had a lot of problems so I got to see totally the other side of something that I never really knew existed. It was a whole other world for me.

Q What do you mean?

A Well, these people live pretty shockingly, really. They've got young kids but they do a lot of drugs and smoke a lot of cannabis and they have plenty of problems. One time I was there the father threatened to stab his wife in front of the kids. The kids were wailing and I tried to pull the knife off him and calm him down.

<blockquote>
" **I just did what I wanted to do. [My parents] were pretty worried about me ..."**
</blockquote>

It was pretty full on - there are a lot of unhappy people out there. Also, the way they got money. It was pretty bad.

Q What did they do?

A The parents would drive us around and we'd pick up receipts from the car park where people drop them, look at the most expensive things on the receipt, go in and shoplift them and then return the stuff and get the cash for them.

Q So the parents organised this?

A Yes - they made money from this too.

Q Did you do other dangerous things?

A I think I took a lot of risks and I was pretty lucky to have come out all right! My friend and I did a lot of shoplifting to get money for drugs. So that was pretty risky because I didn't want to get caught - especially as I am hoping I

<blockquote>26</blockquote>

might join the police force when I finish school!

One time my (then) boyfriend stole a car and he was very drunk. I was frightened to be in the car with him, really frightened, but he wouldn't slow down. We drove around for about two hours. After I got out he crashed the car.

My girlfriend and I also hitchhiked a lot. Once we were running away from her mum because we'd been smoking cannabis and she was angry. I can't believe it now! We were very lucky. We were picked up by truckdrivers and good people - we didn't get a murderer! I've certainly had a lot of luck. I wouldn't take risks like this again if I could avoid it.

Q Did your parents know where you were?

A Not always. Some of the time, but not all of the time. I just did what I wanted to do. They were pretty worried about me and they used to call up my friends and say if you see Sophie tell her we really care about her and would love her to come home, but I was too busy and caught up in doing my own thing to care.

It's a Fact that...

In 1999-2000, about 35 per cent (31,600) of people using refuges and other services provided by the Australian Supported Accommodation Assistance Program (SAAP) were under 24; 19 per cent were aged 15 to 19.

Q You were never concerned about how they might be feeling?

A Not really, to tell you the real truth.

Q So you were basically thinking about your own problems and it didn't occur to you that they might be frantic?

A No, it didn't. I was very selfish. I didn't care about them because I was so mad. I was so angry with them and I've got a pretty shocking temper - I've inherited that from my dad.

Q So were you happy when you were away?

A I was, in the sense that I felt I could do what I

wanted to do when I wanted to. I was answerable to no one but myself. I guess I was happy.

Q Did you go to school during this period?

A I didn't really go to school. I was just partying and didn't really care about school. But I didn't want a job either.

Q Who was the most supportive person to you when you were away?

A I think my best friend's mum at the time, Sylvia. She was absolutely the most supportive. I was staying with her for some of the time and she was really concerned about me but she understood where I was coming from. She was really great.

27

It's a Fact that...

The main reason given by young people in need of housing assistance in Australia is relationship or family breakdown.

An average of 3,470 calls are made to an Australian Kids Help Line each year about homelessness and leaving home, accounting for just over 3.5 per cent of all problem calls.

Q What was so special about Sylvia?

A I guess she just understood me, but she also wanted the best for me. She's good to talk to. She was happy with me staying with them but she also wanted me back with my parents. She talked to them as well but she was concerned for me.

Q What made you return home in the end?

A Sylvia had a big part in that. But I just spoke to my parents and we sort of made agreements and stuff - about me being able to go out when I wanted as long as I told them where I was going. And certain other things about friends and time and stuff.

Q What was it like coming home?

A Good. Weird. Strange in the first little while because I'd come from all this hideous stuff back to my normal house. But I earned my respect and I earned my freedom in the end which is what I set out to get.

Q What do you mean? Do you think your family didn't respect you?

A In a sense, yes. I didn't think they respected the way I thought about things. But when I came back it was different. Immediately different.

Q Did your experiences make you rethink your own family?

A Oh, yeah. It made me realise how really lucky I am. I feel pretty privileged to have the life I do. It's quite easy-going. I don't have a job, even a part-time job, I have enough pocket money, this house - all of it.

Q What was the impact of your leaving on the family?

A They were quite disappointed in me. Hurt and a bit betrayed, I think. I realised, when I got back home, how much I really did hurt my parents and how upset they'd been. I felt pretty bad about that. It really shook my whole family up and I had a different view of them. I hadn't realised how much they loved me. I really hadn't been able to see it.

Q Had this been a huge growth period for you?

A Definitely. I feel as if I've grown a lot more as a person and I've had lots of experiences that have made me who I am now. I'm proud of who I am and I don't regret any of that time at all.

Q In what ways do you feel different?

A I feel very different. It made me see other people's point of view. Seeing how other people live was something I had no idea about before.

Q And you didn't know this beforehand?

A No. Not really. Sometimes you just think all this happens only in the movies. Then you see it. You're in it. It's really horrible.

Q What about things like empathy – sympathy, understanding of other people? Has this deepened in you because of this experience?

A Yes, I think so. At the school I am going to at the moment I've got about four girls who want to beat me up - for stupid reasons. Basically they're

" I feel pretty privileged to have the life I do. It's quite easy-going."

29

A similar neighbourhood to the one Sophie grew up in.

> " ... if my parents had just let me go out more and let me be more independent and listened to what I wanted ..."

all looking for an excuse to bash me. And even though that makes me angry and hurt and I ask myself why do these people dislike me so much for no particular reason, I sort of feel sorry for them.

Q Was there anything that would have made you not run away?

A Yes - if my parents had just let me go out more and let me be more independent and listened to what I wanted and thought.

Q How is your relationship with your parents now?

A We are open. We trust one another. Although I don't like telling everyone everything, I think there are some things you need to keep just for yourself.

Quote from Sophie's mother:

"We think Sophie is an unusually strong person, but she always acts on her emotions and never thinks anything through. We think this experience will make her a much stronger adult and, more able to deal with life."

Q So – any advice for kids like you reading this?

A Advice - gosh! I'd say just think about what you want to get out of leaving home and where it might get you in life. You have to think about where you're going, where you'll stay and how it's going to affect all the people around you. You probably are very loved. I was too angry to see or feel anything other than what I believed - I didn't see how much everyone really loved me at all. But as to the time away, whatever doesn't kill you makes you stronger.

Q What would you call yourself?

A Determined. Stubborn.

Q What do you plan to be when you leave school?

A I'm not really sure, but I'd like to be a writer or an actress or a rock star - possibly all of them!

Q So you would say you were a creative person?

A Yes. But then another part of me likes the idea of being an undercover cop - so what do you make of that?

Q I'd say you like excitement?

A Yes, I do very much. ■

Talking Points

◆ How much do you think Sophie has learned from her experience?

◆ Sophie says she now has respect from her parents. Has she earned this respect? What do you think of her attitude?

◆ Do you agree with Sophie's mother (see panel above) that this experience will make Sophie a stronger adult?

◆ Sophie's parents knew where she was some of the time, but negotiated her return and allowed her to come home voluntarily. Is this the best way for parents to act in these circumstances?

31

It Happened to Lee

Lee, 29, has been taking illegal drugs from the age of 13. He ran away from home, aged 14, after a row with his stepfather and ended up living on the streets. He returned home briefly when he was 16, and again at 17. He has recently become homeless again.

Q What are your memories of family life?

A I lived on a Navy base in Portsmouth until I was three years old. My dad used to get drunk and beat my mum black and blue. One time she got such a beating that, in the middle of the night, she packed our bags, got my sister Carol and me, and ran to her parents' home. We haven't seen my dad since.

Q Did your mum bring you up on her own after this?

A No. She got together with another man fairly quickly and he's the person I have called Dad ever since. Mum was happy with him. We lived on a council estate in Portishead and I remember being taken on holiday in a caravan.

Q And were you happy with your new dad?

A He never showed me any love. I longed to do father-and-son things but that didn't happen. He's a man without emotions.

I never had a conversation with him about anything that mattered. We would just pass each other on the stairs and he'd say, 'All right?' and that was it.

Q Did your mum try to create a happy home?

A My mum is the most loving, beautiful person and she always stuck up for me with my dad. She told him to treat me better. He was never physically abusive but he was spiteful and mean to me. I remember one argument when he turned on me and said, 'You're not my son'. After an argument he would try to make it all right by buying a present, but he'd never apologise. I just saw him as thinking he could buy us off.

> **"I longed to do father-and-son things but that didn't happen."**

It's a Fact that...

Research shows that 100,000 children under 16 (one in nine of the age group) run away from home or care every year in the UK. 77,000 of them are running away for the first time.

Q Did you have good friends at school?

A I had some good mates, but then when I was 13 we moved to a really posh house in a different part of town. This is where things started to go wrong. I was upset at having to leave the friends I had always mixed with. When I used to go back to see them they called me a snob and a traitor for moving away. I didn't hang out with my own age group at my new school. I always wanted to hang out with the older lot - if it meant proving myself by vandalising things, then I did.

Q Were you getting into other kinds of trouble?

A I started sniffing gas when we moved house.

I had my first joint when I was 13. There was LSD and magic mushrooms but speed was my first major drug. Then I started going to acid house events and taking a lot of ecstasy. We lived in the same house as my grandparents and I was able to steal the temazepam my grandmother was prescribed.

Q How did school deal with you?

A I was a problem for school, not interested, breaking the rules, giving them grief, but I was very unhappy and I never felt anyone there cared. I felt picked on by the teachers. I ended up being expelled from secondary school and I saw all kinds of psychologists and counsellors. But nobody seemed to pick up on the fact I wasn't getting on with my parents and that I was very unhappy.

33

> **"I planned to take a bus to London where it was all happening at the time ..."**

me and split my lip. My mum went ballistic. That night I packed my holdall. When my parents were asleep, I stole £80 from my dad's cash box and I just went. It was August and I went to the bus station and waited until morning. I planned to take a bus to London where it was all happening at the time and I'd often been for weekend raves.

Q Did you think of running away at this time?

A I was always threatening to run away. I suppose I wanted to frighten my parents and then one night, while I was still 14, I had a big argument with my dad because I broke a pane of glass in the front door. We had a fight. He head-butted

Q Did you have any idea how you would manage?

A I thought I could find a bed and breakfast and somehow things would just be all right, but it didn't work out that way. The first night I slept in the coach station and then I walked the streets for two days around Victoria.

I then went to King's Cross and asked a few of

the homeless people how they survived. I hung around with them and we begged for money for food. We slept inside the station or just outside in doorways. I met an older guy who had been homeless around King's Cross for ten years. He sort of took me under his wing and looked out for me. I turned to him because he was sort of like a dad.

Q Was there camaraderie among the homeless?

A I chose King's Cross because it's the capital of the dossers. There would be groups of us, about seven or eight. A lot of the young ones were runaways. The best thing about being on the streets is the friends you make. I know people who have been happier living on the street than staying in lonely bedsits.

Q Were there things about the lifestyle that upset you?

A During the first months I was a bit green and not prepared for some of the street scene.

It's a Fact that...

A quarter of young runaways end up sleeping rough, and one in 14 survive through begging, drug-dealing and prostitution.

There were very young girls, absolutely out of it, and willing to do anything with a man for money to fuel their drug habits. And a lot of alcohol was used. It was a strange, insecure world to be in but I can't say I was depressed. When you are living like this some people turn away from you and just treat you like scum, but others were sympathetic.

"I know people who have been happier on the street than in lonely bedsits."

> " In fact I liked the way we were a united group, a bit like a family, on the streets. "

crime. I moved around London doing that, sleeping in parks and places. I started selling drugs: speed and cannabis.

Q Did you see yourself as an outsider at this time?

A I've always felt on the outside so being homeless wasn't much different. In fact I liked the way we were a united group, a bit like a family, on the streets. It's an unwritten rule that you care for each other. When somebody has money they lend it if someone else has none, and then they pay it back when they can. People who have food share with those who don't. Quite a lot of people just look at the homeless as scum, but there's some real decency in the people on the streets.

Q Was it ever frightening?

A I had a time when I moved into three abandoned houses with some older guys. We were always scared of strangers in case they came in demanding money. And

Q Was begging your only way of getting money?

A No. I started getting into shoplifting, taking car stereos, that kind of petty

"I phoned my mum sometimes and she used to beg me to come home."

because most of us on the streets steal a bit to survive we live in constant fear of being caught on CCTV.

Q Did you have any contact with your family?

A I phoned my mum sometimes and she used to beg me to come home. Then when I was 16 I did go home briefly, but I had a girlfriend my family didn't like. My dad told me he thought she was a slag so we moved into a bedsit.

Q How were you living?

A I was using harder drugs so that affected everything. I was 17 and I'd moved on to crack and heroin. My girlfriend couldn't cope with that and I'd had enough of her so we split after about four years.

Q How did you cope after that?

A I went back to my mum's and she had a room all ready for me, as though she'd been waiting. It was good for a while. I got myself sorted, got a job as a labourer and then I went to college and got my City and Guilds in bricklaying. I bought a car, nice clothes.

Q How did your family cope with your drug-addiction?

A I managed to get myself off so that I was totally clean and I knew I wanted to stay that way. I had a really nice life for several years. I went to Greece as a holiday rep. Then a friend got me a job working as part of a team building a house in France. I chose to do this as a way of keeping myself off heroin because at home it was always around, the temptation was always there.

Q What happened when you returned to the UK?

A I started using heroin again almost immediately so I decided to move into a squat. But just the other day we were evicted so, just as when I first ran away, I'm homeless again. ■

Talking Points

◆ How much does this story show how experiences as a child affect you in later life?

◆ Lee left home looking for a better life but ended up living on the streets. Why do you think children believe their problems will be solved by running away? Are there any circumstances when this might be the case?

It Happened to Molly

38

Molly*, an only child, was brought up by her alcoholic, drug-dependent mother and her boyfriend. At the age of 16 she ran away from home.

[* Not her real name.]

Q Do you have happy childhood memories?

A My mum brought me up with a man I thought was my dad - that's what I called him. Life was fine so far as I remember. I was dressed well, there was food on the table and my mum took me to school.

Q So what happened then?

A One day I was home from school, sick, and my mum and the man I called dad had a big row. I am sure, now, they must have both been drunk but I didn't know that then. He threw her across the room, she fell and broke her back. She ordered him out the house and it was then that she told me he wasn't my father. I was about eight at the time.

Q That must have been a big shock for you. Did you find it difficult to adjust to the news and to the fact that he had gone?

A I did miss him. He was good to me and of course it felt very unsettling to know he wasn't my father after all. Mum realised I was confused so she got on the phone to my real dad – she hadn't spoken to him in years – and fixed up for me to have a meeting. I was very nervous. I dressed in my best clothes and got all my school work together to show him. He seemed pleased to know me and then he introduced me to his sister and my half-sister who is eleven years older than I am. That felt good but afterwards he didn't really keep in touch.

Q So how was it with just you and your mum living together?

A It wasn't like that for very long. My mum was moved by the council to a nicer flat and she had a job as a helper at a playgroup. That was a happy time. But then she met Bryan and after that everything went downhill. He was a drug addict and a drunk, and he really got in the way of my relationship with my mum. He was like a tramp, very dirty, and he had lost all but one of his teeth. He was constantly shouting and swearing. I couldn't bear him. I couldn't understand why my mum was doing it and I felt very angry with her.

Q Did your mother know how you felt?

A When she was sober she understood and said she must get herself straight and get rid of him. But as soon as she had a drink she changed and became defensive and it was clear nothing would change. When he moved in with us all the money began to go on drugs so there was very little food in the house. Often we would just share a pizza between three of us. Luckily I was on free school meals so I ate as much as I could then.

Q Did you have to accept that this is how life at home would be?

A I stuck it for about eighteen months but it was horrible, chaotic. There were arguments and drunken shouting.

It's a Fact that...

In the UK a quarter of young runaways sleep rough and one in 14 survive through begging, drug dealing and prostitution.

" ... all the money began to go on drugs ... "

"After a few months I was really missing my mum ..."

So then I went to stay with my grandmother on my dad's side. I had met her through him. While I was with her I got to know my dad's sister and her husband quite well. My gran was great but after a few months I was really missing my mum so I went home.

Q Was it better this time?

A My mum seemed really pleased to see me and she used to come into my room every evening for a chat and to massage my legs because I had growing pains in them and that relaxed them. But one night she was too drunk to do it so Bryan came in and said he would do it instead. But it didn't feel right and then he went too far and rubbed right up the inside of my leg. I don't think he actually sexually assaulted me, although I've blocked out the incident so I can't be sure, but he certainly molested me. I was nine and it just wasn't right and I felt very frightened with things out of control.

Q Did you tell your mother what happened?

A I told her the next day when she wasn't drunk and she was very upset. She kicked Bryan out and kept telling me how sorry she was. I really believed she had made the decision to protect me and I was hoping things would improve at home. But after a few days she let Bryan come back because he said it had all been a mistake. He said he'd been drinking and hadn't realised it was my leg he was rubbing, he'd thought it was my mother's. She chose to believe him.

Q Were you frightened, living at home, that he would molest you again – or worse?

A I was frightened all the time but he didn't ever touch me like that again. He was quite violent in other ways. He would raise his hand threatening to hit me and he threw glasses of water and things at me. I hated him. Everything was terrible with him around. My mother used more heroin and more drink than when she was on her own, and it made both of them completely mad. They would stand in the hall outside my bedroom door screaming at each other and then

It's a Fact that...

Children who run away under the age of 11 are more than twice as likely to be regularly hit by their parents, and almost twice as likely to be bullied at school than children who run away aged between 11 and 16.

" They would stand in the hall outside my bedroom door screaming at each other..."

41

People who, as children, had a history of running away from a young age often say that they struggle to find happiness in later life as well.

they'd barge into my room asking me to take sides in their arguments.

Q Was there anyone to support you?

A I started going to my dad's sister and her husband every weekend. They had a big house and they were always welcoming. Then they suggested I live with them. I was 13 at the time, and when I told my mum I was going she suggested that I make it two months and in that time she would sort herself out so I would be able to go home again. I really liked being with my relatives because they taught me a lot about how life could be pleasant and rewarding and that there are

possibilities in the world. Things I never learnt at home. But then it got difficult because my dad's sister - my aunt - became rather possessive about me. She couldn't have children of her own and she started saying things about my mum that I didn't like. Also she and my uncle were beginning to have arguments. I stayed six months but then I decided I wanted to be back with my mum again. I was 15 and thought perhaps I could handle it.

Q So did you find things were more sorted out, when you went home to your mum?

A At first it was fine. Mum seemed very pleased to have me back.

Bryan was quite in the background. But then it all went bad again. I wasn't allowed in the sitting room most of the time because it was full of people shooting up with needles. My mum used to tell me to leave saying, 'I don't want you to see this'. Then one day I was alone in the place with Bryan and we got into an argument and he said, 'Why did you come back? Your mum and I were fine when you were away.'

Q How did that affect you?

A I was terribly upset and crying when my mum came back. I told her what Bryan had said

> **" I just knew education was the one thing that could save me ..."**

but he denied ever saying it. Again, she chose to believe him. It was then I realised I had to get out. I contacted social services because I'd just turned 16 to see if they could house me, but they said 'no' because I didn't have enough points - enough things in my life that were obviously bad for me - to be eligible. It was a struggle at home studying for my GCSEs with the rows, and not being able to sleep because of the noise and then I was trying to do A' levels. People ask me how I coped with school let alone exams with what I've been through. I just knew education was the one thing that could save me so I was utterly determined to get my GCSEs and A' levels.

One day I couldn't take it any more so I packed my things and told Mum I was going.

Q Did you know what you would do?

A Luckily someone told me about the Camden Under-25s Advice Service in north London. I went down there and met the lady who runs the service and she was brilliant - still is, I see her a lot - she is helpful and caring and supportive. She helped me apply again for housing because I was desperate to get out of home. I was given a hostel place in King's Cross. Frankly it was horrible: dingy and dirty, with a fridge smelling of mould, the odour of smoke everywhere and the room was tiny. But at least I was on my own and that felt good - once I'd got past the drug addicts, prostitutes and pimps on the way to the hostel. Then, after Christmas, the council moved me to a much nicer room further out.

Q Did you see your mother at all?

A I hardly had any contact with her. I didn't want her knowing where I was staying because I felt that somehow she would be trouble.

Q But things weren't so good after a while?

A I was getting very depressed and not sleeping and I often felt I just

> " It was frankly horrible: dingy and dirty, with a fridge smelling of mould ..."

couldn't cope. One day I had a huge panic attack and freaked out completely. The doctor put me on some pills·that made it much, much worse so I stopped taking them. And other difficult things happened. My aunt and uncle got divorced and she then wanted me to turn against him. It felt as though the one family there for me had fallen apart. I really didn't see my dad at all. But in the middle of all this I was moved again and this time to a really wonderful flat in Hampstead where I still live and that made me positively happy.

London is one of the most popular destinations for young runaways.

Q So things changed?

A I started applying to university and I knew I wanted to do something with a social content. I applied to LSE and they interviewed me and even though I didn't get the grades they wanted they still took me and gave me a scholarship. I was thrilled but also terrified because everyone looked so intelligent and the whole place was very awe-inspiring.

Q Did you wish your mother was in your life at this time?

A My mum was always in my mind and as I started Uni I heard she was being evicted from her flat because of drugs. She contacted me and said she really wanted to get away from the people she'd been doing drugs with and she was lucky because the council moved her into a nice flat. She said she wasn't taking her boyfriend and she wanted more to do with me. I thought it all sounded promising, and I

was pleased, but then I found out she was in fact taking Bryan with her and I realised how pointless it was to have any hopes.

Q Do you see your mum now?

A I hardly see her now. I go to Uni, work at weekends in a shop to pay my rent and to be able to afford to go out occasionally. I don't have many friends at Uni because I'm different - nobody would understand my life really, and isn't in a

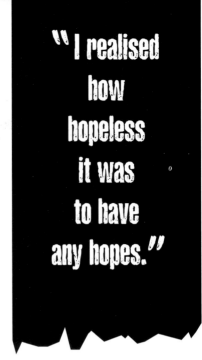

"I realised how hopeless it was to have any hopes."

position to. I'm there to get a degree and the rest doesn't matter. All I want is to create a better future. ∎

Talking Points

◆ What do you learn from Molly's story about the effect of parental break-up on a child? Why do you think her real parentage was concealed from her? How would you feel in her position?

◆ Molly contacted social services for help. Who do you think are the best people to ask for help if you are having problems at home? (For example, relatives, friends, someone at school, social services, children's charities?)

Useful addresses and contacts

UNITED KINGDOM - NATIONAL

ChildLine
A voluntary agency providing a telephone counselling service for children and young people in any kind of danger or distress.

ChildLine, Freepost 1111, London, N1 0BR
24-hour free helpline: 0800 1111
www.childline.org.uk

Barnardo's
A charity that supports young runaways. They offer individual and group activities, focusing on keeping safe and the risks of leaving home. They aim to help families provide a sensitive response when their children return.

Tanners Lane, Barkingside,
Ilford, Essex, IG6 1QG.
020 8550 8822
www.barnados.org.uk

Salvation Army
Offers hostel places to the homeless. Some centres have detox units and rehabilitation facilities. Residents are assigned a key worker to help with problematic issues.

101 Newington Causeway,
London, SE7 6BN
0845 634 4010
www.salvationarmy.org.uk

Message Home
A free confidential message service to let people know you are safe without letting them know where you are.

0800 700 740

Shelterline
A free 24-hour national helpline to help with housing problems.

0808 800 4444

Centrepoint
A national charity for homeless people aged 16-25. It helps people move off the streets and also provides access to education, training and employment.

Bewley House, 2 Swallow Place,
London, W1R 7AA
www.centrepoint.org.uk
020 7426 5300

UNITED KINGDOM - LONDON

Alone in London Service
Providing advice, information and a drop-in service for vulnerable people aged 16-25.

188 King's Cross Road, London,
WC1X 9DE
www.als.org.uk

Camden Under-25s Advice Centre
A drop-in centre offering advice, practical help and guidance on a whole range of issues for young people.

Crowndale Centre, 218 Eversholt Street,
London, NW1

AUSTRALIA

Contact addresses for centres across Australia can be found on the Australian Salvation Army website:
www.salvationarmy.org.au

Glossary

benefit
Money given by the State to people who are unemployed or on low incomes.

camaraderie
Trust and sociability between people, usually friends.

cannabis
A drug which is smoked or eaten.

CCTV
Short for Closed Circuit Television. Cameras which record people on the streets.

class A drugs
The classification for the most dangerous of illegal drugs, such as heroin.

counselling
When people talk about a problem or something that is bothering them with someone trained to help them.

domestic troubles
Problems (sometimes from violence) with one or more members of a person's household.

detox
Short for detoxification. To undergo treatment to come off drugs.

dormitory
A sleeping room with several beds.

dosser
A slang term for a person who sleeps on the streets, or an idle person.

ecstasy
A tablet-form drug with stimulant and hallucinogenic effects.

heroin
A highly-addictive drug made from morphine, a naturally occurring substance taken from the seedpod of the Asian poppy plant. It usually comes as a white or brown powder.

hostel
A place which houses homeless people for a few days or longer.

key worker
Someone who is assigned to a resident of a Salvation Army hostel to help with problematic issues.

probation
A system of supervising and monitoring offenders, as an alternative to prison.

psychologist
Someone who studies people's minds in order to help them.

Salvation Army
A worldwide religious organisation that promotes Christianity and helps the poor.

Samaritans
An organisation that helps people in distress, either over the telephone or face to face.

sanctuary
A place of refuge.

smack
A slang-word for an illegal hard drug, usually heroin.

speed
A stimulant drug.

squat
A building that has been inhabitated illegally by people who do not own or pay rent on it.

temazepam
A drug given on prescription, which has a calming effect.

valium
A drug given on prescription, which has a calming effect.

Index

Getting active!

On your own:
'Children are more likely to run away from home because there is less support in today's community.' Write a short statement to say whether you agree or disagree with this. Draw from your own experience of your neighbourhood.

In pairs:
Imagine you are part of a charity group who runs campaigns and provide support for runaways. Plan a campaign to discourage children running away from home. Research the various ways this could be achieved – different media, school visits, family support, etc.

In groups:
Have a debate on the topic: 'Whatever the home situation children will be worse off if they run away.' Choose people to support each side of the argument and vote as a class on the issue.